ADAGIO for the HORIZON

ADAGIO for the HORIZON

LAURELYN WHITT

Garry Thomas Morse, Editor

EDITIONS

Cover design by Doowah Design.
Cover image from NASA: https://commons.wikimedia.org/wiki/File:M15-162b-EarthAtmosphere-CarbonDioxide-FutureRoleInGlobalWarming-Simulation-20151109.jpg
Photo of Laurelyn Whitt by Rob Lovatt, Keywest Photo–Image by Design Inc.

This book was printed on Ancient Forest Friendly paper.
Printed and bound in Canada by Marquis Book Printing Inc.

We acknowledge the support of The Canada Council for the Arts and the Manitoba Arts Council for our publishing program.

Library and Archives Canada Cataloguing in Publication

Whitt, Laurelyn, author
        Adagio for the horizon / Laurelyn Whitt.

Poems.
ISBN 978-1-77324-025-1 (softcover)

        I. Title.

PS8645.H569A65 2018   C811'.6   C2018-901289-7

Signature Editions
P.O. Box 206, RPO Corydon, Winnipeg, Manitoba, R3M 3S7
www.signature-editions.com

"When we have gone they will not know who they are....
Their world will fade into an endless dusk with no whippoorwill
to call the owl in the evening and no thrush to make a dawn."

— from *The Others: How Animals Made Us Human*
by Paul Shephard

Contents

TAR SONGS: MAESTRO

You have our attention now.

Yellow-slickered figure
raising baton
                    to blue sky.

The clouds pause   hold
          a collective breath

Syncrude's smoke hangs
in clueless waiting.

Something is about to happen
a Hydrocarbon Concerto perhaps, or

the Oiled Duck Symphony.

          "Our desires," the programme
          notes declare, "rarely assume

          desirable form

          but must be extracted
          from the more complex."

Dross remains

after what we desire
is taken away.

It rises, forms
                    lethal boreal lakes.

Swamps the orchestra
laps at our feet.

Visible from space
    you float alone
            sink

    into a final
            packed
            performance.

TAR SONGS: REMNANT

She sits and waits, eyes moving
brush tucked, curled close.

Patches of her coat are missing
her ribs stand out

wrack of the boreal

what remains
once swaths of pine
peat moss

are flayed, the massive pits
gouged.

They gape around her now.

Trucks belching diesel
swarm within

block escape from
another land-locked

leviathan.

The fox sits and waits, pants lightly.
Eyes avid, brush tucked.

Every now and then, drivers toss
a bit of sandwich to the tiny form

below. Laugh as she darts in
to scarf it up. Bet on

who will be the first
to crush her.

TAR SONGS: DAUGHTER/APPARITION

> *"It is happening within our country.*
> *Slow industrial genocide... This is*
> *extinction we are facing."*
> – Mike Mercredi, Dene, Fort Chip

Wading into the waters
of the Athabasca

a slim determined figure
keeps moving –

her back to us. None of us
will ever see her face.

Plumes seep
from impoundments

carry her downstream

leaching cyanide
arsenic, mercury

into the river, fish

mothers

the unborn who never come
yet never leave us.

She disappears
a wraith. The future

wraps around her

a shroud, dead
weight.

TAR SONGS: TAILINGS

"Nearly 2,000 birds die every year from exposure to the ponds." – Kevin Timoney, ecologist

Slurry of crushed rock and
effluents.   Toxic pools fool

caribou, beaver, moose
who bow their heads

to drink. Great undulating

flocks of waterfowl circle
settle

then panic   disoriented

falling under the blasts
of air cannons

the benediction of
floating scarecrows.

They say the bufflehead,
mired, just dove and

never came up.

The wings of others
keep beating

adagissimo
as they try to rise.

We close our eyes.

Still see them.

UNMOORED

Lost to slow
                tumble

September leaves, spent
                        and drifting.

Chilled midnights   turn
                into languorous noons.

Days of the week
dissipate   the year

                bobs
                about

                still afloat.

The ninth month, fulcrum
of the seasons
                unreels.

Some mornings I lie in
a dream of gills
                beached by the surge
                and tug of surf

one lidless eye fixed
on the sun above, mouth

gasping little o's
of oxygen-despair,
                ocean loss.

Often I wake at 2:00 a.m.

to find I have lost
                the plot

and am alone in this
way station
                    stranded

between one story and the next –

aware that the train
has just pulled
                    out.

Those are its tail lights
ahead of me
                    ebbing.

THE TURNING

Against leaden sky, red-and-yellow
balls

a doe rears lightly, reaches drooping
limbs, sour fruit. Twin fawns, spots

fading with summer, pounce
among crabapples.   The prairie

winter is closing upon them.

They skitter before the snap
of bone-cracking

chill. Cold so sharp it
carves chasms in lungs, where

breath disappears forever.

The doe is hungry; the fawns
oblivious. And the woman, who

gazes at horizons, cannot turn away.

Cloud banks bear down on them
roiling. Swirling vortices suck

in wind, fraying ribbons

of geese   stragglers
who have lingered

anxious calls

faint
            in retreat.

ANEMOPHILY

after a photograph by Russell Joslin

A slur of sound, the flutter

of aspens; each limb a clan
of small hands clapping.

In the shoals of tree tops, schools
of silver minnows

ripple, dart
disperse within a lull of air.

Silence soaks her with its sweet
alembic, saturates every pore.

Deep in a trance of listening
she creates a vacuum.

Then *there*:

the rustle of fey winds as they rush
to her, enter

drawn
from all the corners of earth.

LATE OCTOBER

Mesmerized by flickering black-
green rows, early
winter wheat
    they creep

along an endless stretch
of prairie. Drive

the ping and crunch of gravel
road. The dog, head

thrust happily between bucket
seats, rests his greying muzzle

 on her shoulder.

 They ride swells of stubble
 together.

Another massive combine
lumbers in the distance

anchors the implacable
prairie sea.

Soon the fading winter light
will find them.

A coyote breaks from the
brush, stops and turns

fills them with the shifting
currents of her gaze.

MOVING ON

An urgent breeze. Wild geese
dip and rise

in ragged formation. Offer

terse matter-of-fact
honks: head south

or face the consequences.

A few linger
through early winter. Week

by week, they seek the last
patches of open water

until all that remains
are two geese and a single

shrinking pool, an eye closing.
The next morning there is ice

where they were.

VIGIL

Across wind-scoured
furrows of November
over ice-encrusted ground

two figures lope.

It is dark. The moon hangs
low, swollen at the horizon

their rocking bodies shed.
They grow closer

larger now,
               heedless of us. Eddies

of snow swirl and lick. They
are liquid. They are light.

They rise and fall with
the breath of the world   intent

on an unfathomable place

where beings we
cannot imagine

await.

PERIPHERY

In the polar reaches
where the horizon turns

auroral, strange
night creatures

haunt the skies with their
hued existence.

Saturated in bands of light

their heavy breath purls
through a thermosphere

thick with solar winds. They
pace, paw, rear

at shifting curtains

wary senses flaring, eyes
scintillescent wells

      where our own image
      floats, gaze averted

      as though worried
      we will find something

      there   or remember

      the emptiness that contains us.

SGR A*

At the centre of the river of stars
it whirls above us

the end   the edge of the world
we have believed in.

An absence that eats suns
subsists

at the rim of a black hole –
a different horizon

relentless, absolute.

What lies within will never
escape, never reach us

what crosses
from our side
never returns.

Given the magnitude
of our brevity

its presence obsesses us.

What happens beyond that
one-way portal?   what

would there be if we

reckless with the lust of
discovery

    slipped the grasp of our
    galaxy's spiralling arms?

    tumbled across that
                churning threshold?

LOSS OF PERSPECTIVE

Bewildered, the eye scurries
cannot settle
                darts

without relief or
resting place.

Only more distance
in the distance –

      the eye, miserably
      unmoored

      somersaults through space

neither rising nor falling
horizonless.

But up close, too close

it mires
in the blur of the world

      a familiar face
      eclipsed by flesh

      sage-studded hills
      by dirt

bereft of that sweet spot
between near and far

where elements restrain
one another, meet.

Origin of an Origin Story

Something caught in the horizon
                    concatenates

into being
           struggles
to release itself
from the tensile caress of the
unseen
           to inhabit a form.

Beyond the chitter of birth voice
a skirling keen.

What happens within that oasis-
shimmer, those drifting
translucent sheets

        does not stay there.

TAPETUM LUCIDUM

Hiking at night
a man passes a woman

luminous eyes
find hers, enter

shimmering twin
creatures of the deep

adapted to a sunless
realm, and brushed

with iridescence –
a sense of how

things change with place.

Inhabited now, she
courts sight in low

light conditions, leaves
diurnal ways. Notices

her night vision
improves as she ages

increasingly, hears
only nightingales.

Nocturnes.

VISITATION

after a photograph by Gary Mitchell

The hand
of a ghost-lover reaches
through time.

His scent of iron,
faint. Cool metal. Hot

smoky breath. Taste
and touch alternate.

Outside, bare-
         limbed
lilacs
gnarl
at the windows.

Thick walls of hemlock
and fir are lashed

with the ash of
lingering ice fog

Hues of blue flicker
         dissolve

as the winter sun, low
on the horizon, finally

    cracks
    its sallow eye.

LITANY OF LONGING

after a photograph by Douglas Beasley

Longing that survives, excises itself.

Longing of the revenant for what remains.

Adamantine longing that fists itself in defiance.

Longing that aurifies the air.

First longing begins a *pas de deux* with an absent partner –

last longing ends the same way.

Oceans of longing.

Beached and stranded longing.

Longing for an anodyne for longing.

Exclusive longing that chases others away.

Longing of the seed still rising within the tree.

Louche longing that forgets itself and becomes
profligate, prodigal.

Longing gone raucous with desire.

Big-hearted, single-minded longing.

The keep where longing languishes, unseen.

Longing that dives with a loon, finding solace
in other elements.

Riven longing that will not cohere.

Shriven longing unable to forgive itself.

Final longing as it stretches and flaps its wings

seeks species-comfort; summons flock-mind.

ADAGIO: POLAR VORTEX

Before we could name it
we knew it:

relentless, hammering
                            descent.

Huddled in rice-paper houses
through brutal nights
                            stunned
and still
            we barely glowed
            in the dark.

Days, we lost direction
depth

slivered into two-dimensional
beings by wind chill.

Battered sails

we skimmed the scoured
expanses

of Manitoba, Nunavut.

When it hardened
                            vise-like
on Hudson's Bay
                            we heard it

in the crack and boom
of frost
            quakes
                        the
                        sizzle of
                        ice volcanoes

spraying crystals over frozen lakes.

We felt it drop
        further down

over Churchill, where caribou
staggered to their knees.

Where great white bears
loped   and swung their

sleek heads back in alarm
toward what was coming

nearly here, nearly now

then upon us, with

        the weight
        of the Arctic

        ice world
        imminent.

In the minus forties on arrival.

Lasting until spring.

Leaving shards within us.

ADAGIO: THE LAST WAVE

For a time it loomed

      a creature of the mind
      dismissed by it.

Those who knew the seas
rode rogue waves out

      felt how they rose and
      fell, utterly indifferent

      to presence, absence
      of belief.

Now they churn
everywhere, through

oceans and lakes.
      Ten or so, at any
      given moment

scientists say, eyeing
fetch length, wind speed

the surge of currents
in a warming world.

Now the hands of artists
blur and cramp
          as huge walls of

water bear down.

We are all
painting rogues these days

manifestations of
the inhuman human.

We free them from
distant seas, let them

      prowl coastal waters.

Watch our houses
huddle together
              in the vertical

the vulnerable

then drift out to meet them.

      Houses without windows,
      doors.

      The last wave, already
      escaping its frame.

ADAGIO IN CHURCHILL, 2016

Too early or too late, the big males gather on Eskimo Point, sprawl
over rocks, conserving energy. Blanketed by insects and sun. Their
heads – thick, white wedges – punctuate the air heavily, almost in
unison. Swinging up and out, scenting. Imagining seals, walrus.
Dropping down, away.   Improbably, in boreal slow motion,
a female runs by.   Then her pursuer.   He catches her, mounts.

Word of the mating flares through town. At Gypsy's, at the Lazy Bear,
at the Tundra Inn Pub. They huddle around cell phone videos, shaking
their heads. Cree or Dene, Inuit or Métis, Native or not, within an hour,
consensus is reached: this is the first seen in living memory. On land.
In full mid-summer. (Wrong place at the wrong time.) Something's off.

North of here, sea ice has dwindled to a record low. Freeze-up will be
late again this year. At some point, to avoid starvation, bears will slip
into the bay and try to swim for it. Imagining seals, walrus.
Too far away.   Their massive webbed feet churning.

ADAGIO FOR SHISHMAREF

*"The land is going away. I think it is
going to vanish one of these days."*
– Shelton Kokeok

North of Nome, north
of the Bering Strait

Iñupiaq villages   sink
into the Chukchi Sea.

The edge keeps moving.
Shoreline crumbles, as

Morris Kiyutelluk wakes
to the thud and tug of waves.

His house tips
nearly topples.

Come morning, neighbours
will rope and rescue it

from the slushy ledge where
the island ends.   Pull it onto

mushy peat barrens, sodden
and dotted with pools, lakes.

The permafrost has thawed and .
sea ice, two months late, cannot

be trusted. It cracked when
young Norman Kokeok tried to

cross to the mainland. He went
through.

"It should have been frozen
by now," says his father, who

cannot bring himself to leave

and lose it all.

ADAGIO: APOPHASIS ON CAPE BONAVISTA, 2014

They could have been many things.
They were not.

Drawn to the Bonavista that spring
we stood, silenced or

babbling, incoherent; the sea
strewn

with immense shapes. Never
had there been so many.

Heaving gently. Riding the
Labrador current.   Entities

of tongue-numbing beauty
sculpted by colossal hands.

Melting.

Carcasses of huge pelagic
beings, adrift.   A flotilla

of massive ships, hulls
calved, listing.

Residuum of civilization.

      Or (the words none of us
      could force from our lips)

      proof

            that the tipping point
            had been breached.

ADAGIO: CREVASSE

August 2011. No ice in the Arctic.

A polar bear prowls dry land
panting
>
>past the point of
>hunger's burn

into the numbing, the gnawing
at muscle, the dulling of scent

and sight and sound.

Sixty degrees. Only
five hundred miles
>
>*from the Pole.*

The ringed seals are
unreachable. She's found

only seabird nests
the past two weeks

whole colonies
ravaged instantly.

They've flown thousands of miles
to lay eggs, raise chicks.

Now glaucous gulls, barnacle
geese and eider ducks

raise a chaos of cries.

Peck at bits of shells
their shredded nests.

Not a single egg survives.

An entire generation lost.

Another crevasse
                    opens.

CONCH, MID-CONTINENT

In the middle of the continent
a woman lifts a conch shell
                              to her ear

        listens to the moan
        of an ocean.

Down in the valley
                    buffalo
stir, uneasy. Stamp
their feet.

When she raises the conch
                          to her lips
and blows

they swing their great heads
slowly   side to side

as though winter were here

the sweet grasses
deep in snow.

That night I dream the Pacific
breaches

        its shoreline, washes
        east   to meet

        the Atlantic's waters, pooling
        at my feet.

Below, a swell
of canary-gold canola

the indigo-blue of flax.

The odd, disoriented flounder
eyes the North American seabed

with skepticism –

  none of those global warming
  predictions prepared it
                      for this.

SOSTENUTO

"I still look for them. Even though I know they're gone."
— Bill Montevecchi

It was as if a song abruptly failed
or was severed

in that moment, something
in the hummingworld

closed
       fell still

listening for absence
that keeps expanding

a sostenuto of stone.

If you come for their Feathers
do not give yourself the trouble

of killing them, but lay hold of one
and pluck the best.

You then turn the poor bird adrift
skin half-naked and torn off

to perish at his leisure.

The last Great Auk
its feathers soft cerements

stands stuffed, alone on
a solitary herm.

Auk prints surround it.

The moon crescents them out.

॥

*They walked slowly. Jon's bird
went into a corner*

*but mine was going
to the edge of a cliff.*

*I took him by the neck
and he flapped his wings.*

*He made no cry.
I strangled him.*

॥

Granite glinted
in the eyes

of the last pair
                petrified

as their killer smashed
their egg under his boot.

Only the hummingworld
will remember

how the kite of another
species, loosed

soars

jostles with others
in darkening skies.

How we begin to speak
into shadows

when the horizon contracts
                    blinks out.

No Dark Corners

The ghost fish return. Swim out of deep Devonian
waters, eyes smouldering in cool seas. Their bodies
iridesce, silver-blue flecked with white like the
mollusk-studded lava caves they leave.

> *Large, luminescent eyes, an alien green,*
> *kept looking at me…*

Sculling splayed fins, they fan dance in oceanic
currents, gone vertical, head down, as hypotheses
net them: the missing link? a walking fish? the tie
between land and sea? Rewards are offered, signs
posted. Wanted: alive or dead.

> *Wherever I went its eyes followed.*

Fixed on precision, we count the hours this remnant
of four hundred million years takes to die. Fighting
the line. Lactic acids building. Going blind in the light.

> *By 3:30 pm it was lying belly-up, its fins*
> *and gill covers making agonized movements.*

Slow asphyxiation, it bakes in a tub. No dark corners
to hide in, mouth agape.

> *To this day, no coelacanth has survived*
> *the trauma of capture.*

Labs, museums, aquaria, keen on specimens
of their own, court the next extinction:

> *I don't see why there might not be*
> *another population of coelacanths*
>
> *somewhere.*
>
> *I just hope we never find them.*

REUNION: HOLY ANGELS RESIDENTIAL SCHOOL

drawn from a photograph by Ian Willms

After forty years, no voices:

only something that buzzes
erratically, at the sill.

Rorschach stains peel
on the ceiling, residue

of dreams that crept
into morning.

The shadow of a cross
cast by the failing sun

burns on, an afterimage

joining men in robes whose
portraits hang askew
on fleur de lis'ed wallpaper

gilt blooms billow —
musk of memory
incense of regret.

Someone has dusted the long
wooden table. Bibles, hymnals

and a Dene dictionary sit
upon a frayed altar cloth   beside

Blessed Kateri Tekakwitha

smallpox scars vanquished
by death.   In the corners

of the room, skitters
whispers.

The former students

                        file in.

THE ROAD HOME

after Robert Houle's paintings of his confinement
in Sandy Bay Residential School

In a dormitory of quiet boys
one in the corner might be

missed.

When the full moon finds him
through paint-flecked windows

its glaucous eye
huge and unblinking, catches

    small, scuffed sandals, carefully
    aligned under his bed

creeps along the metal frame
    up a thin brown spread.

    Again the Cross, dangling
    on a knotted cord. The heavy
    black robes.

He lies limp, stifles every breath

begins to walk the long road
home, hears

nothing, sees
nothing, feels

only the raptor
circling overhead

the bewildering certainty

of what will happen
night after night.

Pahgedenaum,
        o please
pahgedenaum: (let it go

let it go

let it fly from
        your mind).

WOMAN WHO GAZES AT HORIZONS

"Here is the land of our progenitors,
and here…their bones; they left them as
a sacred deposit; …it is dear to us."
– George Harkins (Choctaw)

They say she rode off with some man
       on horseback
left her husband and children behind

disappeared one day into the wild
       blue yonder
swallowed up by the maw of sky.

Not a one of us ever seen her again
       but we heard
she was heading for home, going

back, along the trail of tears to
       Mississippi, to
her land up north in Tishomingo.

      ❊

They say she kept turning back
       as she left
imagining each grandchild she'd

never see; that she never did stop
       haunting
that horizon, eyes full of distance

gazing west. See how she is in this
       photograph?
Standing on a wooden bridge, all

dressed in black? Her body is
       crossing
but her head turns back. Hand

raised, shade against the sun. Look

at the way
she waits, searching for someone.

EMPIRE

"The white race...to which the civilized people of Europe
belong...is also superior to others."
– Georges Cuvier, naturalist

It is an art mostly
unknown. With

the mind's eye

you create an entire being
from a fragment of bone.

Envision coherence, how
form holds parts together

how this and earlier
worlds must be

if creatures such as these
are to inhabit them.

Move on to imagine serial
species extinctions

worlds destroyed by
catastrophes, epidemics.

Civilized worlds and
savage ones. Races

separate, unequal, distinct.

Colonized worlds.
Colonized bodies.

In his mind's eye
Cuvier did this.

A DARK TICKLE PASSAGE

*after David Blackwood's etching
"Uncle Eli Glover, Moving"*

There are dreams where horizons
do not surround
but fill us. This is one. The arc

of the coast no longer
cradles my boat. My house

is afloat on the open sea

caught between islands,
outports   hauled by a

skiff of slicker-clad
men   keeping
                their distance

all of them looking away.

They have not spoken since this
started.   Nothing in them

stirs or wants to be said.

A leaden sky sinks
into ocean swell.

No land in sight.

Only two dark
elements

eclipsing one another.

HEADING OUT

> *"I think of things as beginning rather than ending."*
> – Alex Colville

Slack water. Gulls streel
from the departing skiff

    dismayed souls

    haunt the rim
    of the continent
        with screeches, wails

    circle in faint reprise

da capo, da capo
        repeatedly…

        Beyond, in the offing

        an island no one has
        imagined or seen.

        Something finning
        through long, flat sighs
        of sea

        gains speed as it approaches

        then sheers   with a sudden
        sleight of fin

        disappears.

The skiff's bow skips
dances, skims

    over shoals, heading for
    deep water.

Just ahead, the shimmer
of another horizon

the glim of an ice field, or perhaps

an oncoming wave.

ASHORE

Between Ireland's Eye
and the Horse Chops

North Atlantic squalls
slap at a rim of rock.

A lighthouse beam sluices
sight.

Fixed upon it

you ride the whelm
of night in, one-minded

       while capelin spawn themselves
       roiling, in a final

       surge up, past receding
       waters, to tumble

       within the caul of moonlight.

There, curled and tucked among
spalls of shells, splintered

timbers, your every sense
ebbs to touch.

The gentle spell
of the haptic as it takes you.

      The island
          nudges, fastens
                   itself.

CONTACT

Every night they appear:
rising and diving

Minke and Humpback
the occasional sperm whale

flank the Horse Chops
skirt English Head.

Their bodies, dark needles
agleam with moon

stitch blue-black veils of
sky to Trinity Bay, stay

frayed horizons, knitting
the elements together.

Come morning, only
traces   endless seams

the swells of an
            emptied harbour.

GHOST FLOWER

Beneath the boreal canopy's
stuttering celluloid   deep

flickering greens
                    that staccato
of shadow
            and light
                        they surge

up to stand among us
                        phantoms
                                    upon erect stalks
stretched thin
with urgency
                up until their fluted heads
slump.

Company.

Come with the sedative
        of simple presence

the solace
        of powdered root

introducing themselves modestly
(aka *Indian Pipe*, aka *Fairy Smoke*)

medicine that induces
calmness, clarity

            that takes us back
                        from the edge.

Liminal beings
        doing liminality's work:

            bringing otherworlds
        into this one.

CLUMPS

Through wooden rooms of
an outport house

the newcomer staggers, in nearly
      drunken deliberation.

      Floorboards, warped
      with weather, worn
      with use
            slant up

      jolt the right foot
                  down
      jostle the left.

      ※

Seduced in the barrens

by assumptions of
stability, a prairie flatness

she flounders
      off-path

      among creeping
      berries, mosses, densely
      woven mats of shrubs

      every step a risk or
      gamble, a likely plunge

      through boggy oblivion

      into the waiting mouth
      of rock.

Breaks
      into panicked

high-steps   tries to

find the way back.

Doubts that can happen.

⁂

She leans forward into
islander speech, listens

    and reels.

    Ears wide open to
    loss of equilibrium.

Rides the pitch and
    yaw of dialect

      as island
      cadences

        rock the cradle
        of meaning.

Comprehension   discontinuous
arrives
      when it does

    in small, delayed   clumps.

SALVAGE

In the landwash
                              lies
the meaning of
                              everything.

I set off to have a look
to comb litter left

by the heave and swash
of sea

to canvass the forgotten
the discarded

the taken:

        one cracked oar, a child's
        faded flip-flop, some frayed
        blue twine, bits of cork
        from a fishing net

carried in on a procession
of waves, precious gifts

beached
abandoned.

Dislocated, they dry
bleach, become shells of

themselves, broken
thinning.

        Why not leave it at that?

        The ocean would – to
        randomness, decay

        chaotic scatter.

But what of the old woman

the scavenger, limping
the shoreline?

> She imagines a child
> who sees that cork

> floating in twine near
> a rowboat.

> He reaches for it with an
> oar then slips
>   losing a flip-
>   flop.

Did the boy survive or become
entangled by twine?

Does this woman with the sack
have any answers?

ROUNDING THE COAST

He slides
over brindled shallows

skirting sinkers, leans
into the dory's oars

pulls
against the North Atlantic

sinewed, flexing
        currents catch
then release him.

            How long has he courted
            this tense, essential line

            where a heart of
            black rock is tethered

            to the thrum of sea?
            where land curves

            and sags with the
            weight of water?

Starrigans stud cliff faces
stark, intent

nearly spent
from not letting go.

Beneath him, the tide
quickens

            he listens for the rote
            of the sea, its song of
            return

            the surf as it breaks.

Fog coils and snakes over
Trinity Bight, smothers

lighthouses, envelops docks

    isolates a woman
    in the landwash

    who walks, waits.

Beyond her
        stuttered
        with gull cries

      the harbour
            draws him in.

MAKING DO

for Leon Ivaney

In the glass of my upstairs window
the world goes wavy, uneven. I watch
my neighbour, coming on ninety, totter
through his garden, tending potatoes,
carrots, beets. I worry that the lumpy
earth will fool him. But old sailors, it

seems, never lose their sea legs. He
tips then catches himself: a lurching
rush, a quavery halt, onward. Looks to
straddle a deck again, sailing choppy
seas.

Later, he shows me photographs
of the outport in its prime. Rows
of fish flakes. A smiling couple
in Sunday best. Some time ago
an accident took her. You were
together how long?
                    Fifty years
I draw in a sharp breath.
                    He grips
the table. Winds pick up. The
waves quicken. We ride out the
pitch   fight to stand erect.

Endurance, it comes to me
(he bends precariously
the community ticks on)
may simply be serial recovery

as body and heart just make do.

FOG-LOOM

Hunched over teacups at the kitchen table,
my neighbour and I study opacity. It billows
and swirls past the window, saturates
the cove.

"I'm the loneliest man in the world," he says,
his wife of many years, lost. From a worn
wooden chair he ponders headstones in the
graveyard. Photographs fill the room. Spill
across the table.

The moaning foghorn pinions us. Two small
flecks in a Sung Dynasty landscape, eclipsed
by mountains. Absorbed by the world that
surrounds us, we neither choose, nor refuse,
perception.

In his grief I find my father's, heavy and huge.
Floundering. Now, as then, my hand moves
toward his.   Pauses   at the size of her
absence.

BERTH

So little is said by
the red saltbox
house that stands
tall, alone at the
mouth of the bay.
It clings to earth
with eloquence
won from fierce
gusts, pervasive
salt-mist.

Nothing must be
said of it. All that
can is this. First
thing seen from
open water. Last
thing to disappear.
There when the
foghorn pauses.
When immense
silence settles,
sinks.

HORIZON: THE CHILD'S INVOCATION

> *for containing us without restraining us*
> *for eluding our grasp*

Arc of human perception, embrace
of what is known

where senses
wash and ebb

strand themselves.

> *for drawing circles around us*
> *for enfolding us in the world*

Rim of the nest we try
to reach, far edge

of the universe.
From it

we learn
what is

what cannot leave us.

HORIZON: INVOCATION AT MID-LIFE

for responding, without needing us
for never leaving us out

Tucked discreetly into
the world,   a given

never relinquished

the crucial assumption
from which all else proceeds

within it, we linger.

for joining us as we go
for not being fixed

Portable place, guarding
against   drift.

Like shadow or skin
making us centre.

It knows nothing of the great
stain of forgetting,

abandonment.

HORIZON: A PARTING INVOCATION

for embracing us while drawing us on
for not being illusory

Eclipsing borders and
fences, setting
limits without constraints

still   there

when we close our eyes.
There, where everything is

more than it seems.

for preparing us for the end
for holding nothing back

It waits until we are ready
sends out warnings, dreams.

Gives us time
to adjust

lay in provisions.

This is where imagination
falters, fails and
is redeemed.

ROSA, STRENGTH

after a photograph by Elizabeth Siegfried

Gravity's cupped hand opens
giving her up.

Perched in a chair, fledgling
on the cusp of flight

she clings to moments
where risk lives –

commits the world
                        to memory.

Each visit, there is less of her
but more that is Rosa:

at ninety-eight, the inessential
has been shed

she is distilled.

Last night, a young woman
on horseback, she chased

the limits, reached them.

This morning, she still
clutches mane, hears

the horse's laboured breath
their warm bodies
                        one.

Wonders where she is

on which side
of the horizon?

MAN, ROWING

after a sculpture by Larry Williamson

Ahead a line

    recedes, pulling sky
        into sea

    the shore where blues meet.

Waves break and subside
on beaches of air.

In pursuit, a man in a boat
rowing intently.

    Eyes fixed, fiercely committed

    tireless as stars that reel
    and blur above

    he has left us.

Never to notice
how the world retreats

or that he himself
has grown so small

he merges in the offing
with the line he pursues

    so small we fail to see

    how he flings his arms
    wide open

CLEARING THE GRAVES

*"We actually drove past her. There was
nothing there. All her things were gone.
I was devastated."* – Ashley Marshall

I walk among the dead: their
ordered rows, manicured lawns,
    weedless perfection.

The same neatly aligned dominoes,
identical urns at their heads, are
    not the same.

On each plot, with quiet shrines,
the living inveigh against
    assimilation:

    beside the child who loved bears
    and beetles, a young man in the sand
    with a surfboard

    nearby, two grinning grandparents
    ride Harleys

    a bottle of Cholula hangs
    over my parents.

One day a sign appears:
    *Unauthorized Items
    Will Be Confiscated*

soon stuffed toys join
catcher's mitts, torn
photographs, broken mugs

    a smouldering farrago
    in the burn pit

as living and dead mingle
together, disoriented.

The same and
not the same.

ENTROPY

(fr. Gk, entropia, "a turning toward")

Sparse burials over
random hills –
   seeds flung to the wind.

Aimlessness pervades graves
chosen by loved ones:

   she'll like it here among the trees
   he'll appreciate this view
   we'll always find them by that rock.

No paths link entangled roots
of fir, pine, cedar.

   The sunken rectangles lie alone

   except where a handful of veterans
   are mustered together.

Here a board, blank and
weathered   there a head-
               stone

   its worn shape, a trace of
   intent, sets it apart from
   rubble.

Sown scantily among the old
are the new
   in white gravel, plastic flowers.

If not for their presence, this would be
a doubled absence
   the cemetery of a ghost town.

Decades pass, settle
into centuries
    bodies come and go.

The mountains never pause
    in their watch.

Weeds and thistles rustle, catch thirstily
at my ankles, tentative, waiting, wanting
    to get on with it.

LAKE BONNEVILLE

Mountains are fading on the Wasatch Front.

Serrated edges grow dull, slopes sag, bits of
boulder tumble into talus. Each spring they melt

then avalanche, easing back onto benches where
an immense lake once lapped

companionably.

Increasingly it is the lake they remember.

The valley that is not a valley no longer cradles
the squalling warmth of bodies.
                                     Now a lakebed

whose pluvial waters rose and fell for millennia
before climbing the slopes
                              that brush of shoreline

repeats a history of orogeny – how mountains
first sprang up and shook themselves

free of earth   rupturing the sky.

How they rimmed the Great Basin to contain
it, then let it go.

How a world so
long in the making
                     simply vanishes.

RELIQUARY

After she died, he spread poems on their bed.

Every morning he read and arranged them,

small panes on a window she still passed.

Days fell away, the weeks, the months. He

gathered them in his arms, pressed them to

his chest. Setting one here, another there,

taking them from room to room. Anxious

to find the right place.

Only the poems had given her up.

They live in a drawer he never touched

again. Where even now they slip into

alphabets of bone. Fade like shadows

fallen into light, or the purling of distant

voices.

IMPERMANENCE

Living widens the passage
of time, inflects it

with subtle distinctions.

      We sense the insubstantial
      in *evanescent,* find

      fleeting passes more swiftly
      than we wish, that what lacks

      lasting appeal
      is *ephemeral.*

So the world humours
perception
              ontology and its
                    remorseless
                    absence of us

                    is kept at bay.

Leaving us vaguely aware that
the present is past

that by the time we perceive
      perception is over.

IMMERSION

"To see is to forget the name of the thing one sees."
– Paul Valery

To be oblivious to the spider
at the centre and know only

the silken thread of the web.

To see
until we are swallowed whole

until centripetal pull weakens
and we spiral down
into a vision of being
                    blinded

by intensity, the density of
the sun.   Losing ourselves

in the constricting pupil, the
eidetic grip of memory –
a view down the rim of a well

to where the wild effulgent
heart of a world lies beating, lies

nearing enlightenment

to become the light, the lotus
in the mind

at the end of the tunnel

HOSHI JINJA

*"Many 'Hoshi Jinja' [Star Shrines]... are still revered
despite the fact that the meteorites they once sheltered
have long since been removed or stolen."* – Dan Snow

Fallen stone from another world

           within thin
      black fusion crust
metallic flakes

          glitter

scattered stars
      held close, in
           depths of space.

Seared upon that surface, a
cosmic thumbprint or two

marks passage
through the atmosphere.

An extraterrestrial
survivor

whose arrival took
six billion years

to complete.

Fallen stone
born of nothing

embedded in a slab
of slate.

Eyes lowered, gaze
averted

seduced
by recondite rock

we would
    would not   approach

            what remains

            this nest
            this portal

still thrumming
with sanctuary.

SOLO, SOLSTICE

On the other side of the horizon
on the longest day

the first thrush
                awakens

cocks his head in
contemplation   one black eye
then the other skewers the sky

the canopy stirs, without song

       until the opening finds him
       an interval to enter, animate

       that singular shift

       in pitch as music rises
       senses itself

       finds its way out, and in.

He sings a first note
       replete   wanting

       resonant A of the oboe
       before the concert begins

falls silent

       until all the rest rise in response
       in desire or empathy or some

       Hallelujah

at that, the sun pauses overhead
       transfixed by this Great
      Cacophony

when the whole manic avian

orchestra tunes up

expecting
another performance.

NOTES

"Tar Songs"
"Tar Songs" is a poetic sequence based on selected images from Ian Willms's photographic essay of the tar sands, "As Long as the Sun Shines." The essay can be accessed at: http://www.ianwillms.com/oilsands#1

"Tar Songs: Remnant"
The story of this fox comes from Mike Mercredi, Dene, from Fort Chip.

"Sgr A*"
Sgr A*, or Sagittarius A-star, is believed to be the site of a supermassive black hole at the centre of the Milky Way galaxy.

"Tapetum Lucidum"
The Latin term "tapetum lucidum," or "bright tapestry," refers to a layer of tissue in the eye which reflects light and causes the eye to glow at night. It is characteristic of many vertebrates (though not humans) – especially nocturnal carnivores and deep sea animals. It is responsible both for superior night vision and for the phenomenon known as eyeshine.

"Adagio: The Last Wave"
This poem is drawn from a painting by J.D. Slack and Terry Daulton. The italicized phrase is from Stefan Helmreich, in a lecture given at Memorial University, Newfoundland, in the fall of 2015 on "The Water Next Time."

"Adagio for Shishmaref"
This poem is based on an article by Steve Visser and John Newsome on CNN: "Alaskan village votes to relocate over global warming" (August 18, 2016)

"Adagio: Crevasse"
This poem is indebted to the stunning work of photographer Camille Seaman on the loss of polar ice in *Melting Away*. The italicized lines are taken from her description of her experience photographing in the Arctic, recounted in the TED blog, "Touching the Directions."

"Sostenuto"
In North America, the Great Auk thrived on Funk Island, off the coast of Newfoundland. Prized commercially (primarily for their feathers) by Europeans, the Great Auk was hunted to extinction on Funk Island by 1800. The last known surviving colony, on the island of Eldey near Iceland, was

then hunted to extinction by the museum industry. The Great Auk had been used as a source of subsistence by the Beothuk, whose extinction occurred soon thereafter.

Passages in italics are drawn from *The Great Auk* by Errol Fuller.

"No Dark Corners"
The italicized lines are from *A Fish Caught in Time* by Samantha Weinberg.

"The Road Home"
The title of this poem is drawn from Robert Houle's art exhibition, *Robert Houle: enuhmo andúhyaun (the road home)*. "Pahgedenaum" is an Anishinaabemowin term meaning "let it go from your mind."

"Woman Who Gazes at Horizons"
Beginning in the 1830s, a number of the Indigenous nations in the southeastern portion of what had become the United States were forced to "remove" west of the Mississippi River. The colonists wanted their traditional homelands but not the People whose homelands they were. A number of the Choctaw who were "removed" did not stay that way. They returned to the land that would not leave them. This poem is about one of them. Her English name was Rebecca Bradshaw.

"A Dark Tickle Passage"
A tickle is a narrow salt-water strait that is difficult or treacherous to navigate. (Dictionary of Newfoundland English)

"Ghost Flower"
Information regarding this plant is drawn from herbalist Sean Donahue.

"Salvage"
The italicized lines are from Tom Dawe.

"Immersion"
This poem is drawn from a photograph by John Acurso.

"Hoshi Jinja"
This poem is based on "Star Shrine," a work by Master dry stonewaller and environmental/assemblage artist Dan Snow. See his book, *Listening to Stone*.

ACKNOWLEDGEMENTS

I am grateful to the editors of the following publications in which these poems first appeared, sometimes in different versions:

The Antigonish Review for "Adagio: Apophasis on Cape Bonavista, 2014," "Adagio: Crevasse," and "Ghost Flower" • *ARC* for "A Dark Tickle Passage" • *Conclave: A Journal of Character* for "Woman Who Gazes at Horizons" • *ellipsis...literature and art* for "Rosa, Strength" • *Event* for "Fog-Loom" and "Periphery" • *Grain* for "Adagio in Churchill, 2016," "Adagio for Shishmaref," "Ashore" and "Solo, Solstice" • *Isthmus* for "Man, Rowing" • *Kindred* for "Berth" and "Reliquary" • *The Nashwaak Review* for "No Dark Corners" • *Off the Coast* for "Making Do" • *Prairie Fire* for Tar Songs: "Tailings" and "Daughter/Apparition" • *PRISM International* for Tar Songs: "Maestro" and "Remnant" • *Room* for "The Road Home" • *The Stillwater Review* for "Unmoored" • *Cultural Studies* for "Adagio: The Last Wave"

and to the anthologies:

{Ex}tinguished & {Ex}tinct: An Anthology of Things That No Longer {Ex}ist, edited by John McCarthy (Twelve Winters Press: Sherman, Illinois 2014) for "Sostenuto," "Sgr A*," and "Lake Bonneville" • *Fading Light: Open to Interpretation*, George Slade and Jacqueline Kolosov, Judges (Taylor & O'Neill: St. Paul, Minnesota, 2013) for "Anemophily" and "Immersion"

For fellowships and residencies that assisted in the completion of this book, I am grateful to the following: The English Harbour Arts Centre, the Churchill Northern Studies Centre, the Gushul Studios of the University of Lethbridge, the Manitoba Arts Council, Sage Hill, and the Wallace Stegner House. Warm thanks as well to Don McKay for his support and encouragement; to Karen Haughian and Garry Thomas Morse at Signature Editions, for all that they do so well; and to Alan Clarke, who sustains me, undeterred by distance and that line on the map.

ABOUT THE AUTHOR

Laurelyn Whitt's poems have appeared in various, primarily North American, journals including *Nimrod International*, *The Malahat Review*, *Puerto Del Sol*, *PRISM international*, *The Tampa Review*, *ARC*, *Rattle*, *Descant*, and *The Fiddlehead*. The most recent of her four poetry collections, *Tether* (Seraphim Editions), won the 2013 Lansdowne Prize for Poetry. She is also the author or co-author of three non-fiction titles. She has a PhD in Philosophy of Science from Western University, immigrated to Canada in 2007, and is a Professor of Native Studies at Brandon University. Currently, she divides her time between Manitoba and Newfoundland.